ZERO-SUGAR RECIPES COOKBOOK

By Coker Rebecca

ZERO-SUGAR RECIPES COOKBOOK

Discover a collection of 80 deliciously simple sugar-free recipes, carefully crafted to satisfy your cravings while keeping sugar at bay. Plus, take advantage of a 30-days meal planner to help you stay on track and enjoy a healthier, sugar-free lifestyle.

Coker Rebecca

COPYRIGHT

TABLE OF CONTENTS

INTRODUCTION

Welcome to the Healing Journey

Has it ever occurred to you to live without having to worry about insulin levels and blood sugar increases all the time? Introducing David, a middle-aged guy who used the Zero-Sugar Diet Cookbook to start a life-changing journey. David, confronted with the overwhelming truth of his diabetes, decided to start over and explore the culinary delights that would eventually serve as his medication.

David learned how to create scrumptious, filling meals without sacrificing taste or nutrition in the center of his kitchen. He found his way to vitality by following the pages of the Zero-Sugar Diet Cookbook, which led him to a world of healthy ingredients and creative meals.

David saw his diabetes gradually reverse with each thoughtfully chosen meal, taking back control of his health and wellbeing. He accepted the bounty of nutrients and flavors, and the necessity of high sugar and insulin became less apparent.

The Zero-Sugar Diet Cookbook evolved into more than just a recipe book through the prism of this culinary adventure; it also became a story about David's successful transition to a sugar-free, satisfying life. This is a story of empowerment, where food took on a purpose beyond mere satiety and evolved into a force for change. Take a savory journey with David and use the Zero-Sugar Diet Cookbook as a roadmap to a happier, healthier tomorrow.

1.1. An Overview Diet Cookbook

Choosing to adopt a zero-sugar diet is a commitment to regaining health and vigor in the fast-paced world of modern eating, where sugary temptations are everywhere. Presenting "The Zero-Sugar Diet Cookbook," our goal is to take you on a culinary journey beyond restriction, embracing a world of flavorful combinations, healthy foods, and the strength that comes from choosing food with awareness.

Unprecedented quantities of added sugars in our diets have been linked to a wide range of health issues, including metabolic disorders and obesity. This cookbook is a goldmine of dishes that expand the possibilities of a sugar-free lifestyle, making it a beacon for anyone looking to follow a better, sugar-free path.

You will find a multitude of delicious recipes inside these pages that are skillfully prepared to stimulate your palate without the use of refined sugars. Every recipe on this page, from delicious breakfast foods to filling lunches, opulent dinners, and decadent desserts, is proof that flavor and culinary enjoyment don't have to suffer when following a zero-sugar diet.

We start this trip with a better comprehension of how sugars affect our health. We investigate the obscure origins of added sugars, illuminating the frequently disregarded offenders that smuggle themselves into our regular diets. Equipped with this knowledge, we next set out on a delectable quest to discover healthy, organic substitutes that enhance our food without sacrificing nutritional content.

"The Zero-Sugar Diet Cookbook" is a comprehensive guide to redefining your relationship with food, not just a cookbook. With helpful hints, meal planning techniques, and a celebration of a variety of nutrient-dense, high-quality ingredients, our mission is to enable you to make decisions that align with your health objectives.

With the intention of living a life unencumbered by sugar, allow this cookbook to accompany you on a journey to rediscover the pleasure of eating. Every dish is a step toward taking back control of your health, whether your goal is to lose weight, maintain a stable energy level, or just maintain a healthy lifestyle. Welcome to a world where eating sugar-free becomes a source of vitality, balance, and most importantly, delicious delight, and where every meal is a celebration of health.

Welcome to An Extensive Look at What a Zero-Sugar Recipes Means

In a world where luxury is frequently accompanied by sweetness, the idea of a zero-sugar diet presents itself as a revolutionary method for recovering vitality, health, and general well-being.

Fundamentally, the goal of a zero-sugar diet is to free people from the negative consequences of consuming too much sugar by purposefully removing additional sugar from their diet.

Hidden sugars, sometimes concealed in processed meals, drinks, and even ostensibly healthful options, are a common occurrence in the modern diet. A zero-sugar diet is a clear break from this pervasive tendency, encouraging people to read labels carefully, find hidden sugar sources, and adopt a lifestyle that puts an emphasis on eating whole, unprocessed foods.

This is not just about cutting out processed sugars from your diet. It includes choosing full, nutrient-dense foods over processed, high-sugar options with an awareness of one's carbohydrate intake. The cornerstones of a zero-sugar diet are fruits, vegetables, lean meats, and healthy fats. They provide a wide range of tastes and textures while providing the body with vital nutrients.

Realizing the harmful effects of added sugars on general health is one of the main drivers behind switching to a zero-sugar lifestyle. In addition to causing weight gain and metabolic issues, eating too much sugar has been connected to insulin resistance, inflammation, and a higher chance of developing chronic illnesses. A proactive move toward reducing these dangers and promoting long-term health is adopting a zero-sugar diet.

The path to go sugar-free is not about restriction, but rather a celebration of creative cooking and a rediscovering of the sweetness found in whole foods. This cookbook functions as a reference, providing an abundance of recipes that highlight the diverse range of flavors that may be produced without the use of processed sugars. All of the recipes, which range from tasty breakfast options to savory dinners and delightful sweets, prove that a low-sugar diet does not have to sacrifice flavor or satisfaction.

In the end, adopting a zero-sugar diet is an opportunity to rethink how you interact with food, to appreciate the sweetness that is inherent in the natural world, and to undergo a significant transformation toward a life full of vitality, energy, and long-term well-being. With the help of this cookbook, o on a trip where the lack of sugar turns into a source of empowerment and discover the real meaning of a tasty, nutritious, and sugar-free existence.

1.2. Getting Around the Zero-Sugar Recipes

A Culinary Journey of What to Put in and Take Out

Starting a zero-sugar recipes involves making the decision to rethink your relationship with food and adopt a healthy, nourishing way of living. We explore what to include and what to leave out in "The Zero-Sugar Diet Cookbook," offering guidance to anyone looking to cut added sugars from their diet.

Foods to Add:

1. Fresh Fruits: You can enjoy the inherent sweetness of fresh fruits like berries, apples, melons, and citrus fruits while avoiding additional sugars. These offer a pleasing sweetness without the negative effects of processed sugars, in addition to providing necessary vitamins and minerals.

2. Veggies: The foundation of a low-sugar diet, veggies are full of fiber, antioxidants, and a variety of minerals. A varied and nutritious dish includes leafy greens, cruciferous veggies, colorful peppers, and other ingredients.

3. Lean Proteins: A balanced and fulfilling diet is ensured by including lean protein sources such as fish, chicken, tofu, and lentils. Proteins are essential for sustaining the health of muscles, encouraging fullness, and regulating blood sugar levels.
Whole Grains: Choosing whole grains instead of refined grains gives you fiber, complex carbs, and long-lasting energy. Brown rice, quinoa, and oats are examples of whole grains.

4. Healthy Fats: Nuts, seeds, avocados, and olive oil become vital ingredients that give food depth and taste. These beneficial fats enhance general wellbeing and aid with satiety.

Foods to Avoid:

1. Added Sugars: Removing added sugars is the main goal of a zero-sugar diet. This comprises high-fructose corn syrup, brown sugar, white sugar, and other sweeteners that are frequently used in processed meals.

2. Processed Foods: Sugars are often hidden in a variety of forms in processed foods. Avoiding pre-processed meals, sugary cereals, and packaged snacks will help prevent hidden sugars and encourage a diet high in whole foods.

3. Sweetened Beverages: Fruit juices, sodas, and sweetened teas are among the sugar-laden beverages that greatly increase the intake of sugar. Water, herbal teas, and infused water turn into a cool, sugar-free substitute.

4. Sugary Condiments: Sugar is frequently added to ketchup, barbecue sauce, and salad dressings. If you stick to your zero-sugar diet, you can still enjoy flavor by using homemade or sugar-free alternatives.

5. Sweets and Desserts: Although traditional desserts are heavy in sugar, adopting a zero-sugar lifestyle does not entail sacrificing sweetness. The cookbook provides creative dessert recipes that let you enjoy a guilt-free pleasure using natural sweeteners like monk fruit or stevia.
With every recipe in "The Zero-Sugar Diet Cookbook," you may experience the colorful, tasty possibilities that come with adopting a diet devoid of added sugars. Explore the delight of a sugar-free culinary journey through these pages, where each taste is a celebration of vitality, health, and the delightful simplicity of natural flavors.

CHAPTER 2

The Ultimate Zero-Sugar Recipes

20 Breakfast Recipes

Omelette and vegetables

Cooking time: 10 minutes   **Portion size:** One omelette

Ingredients:

- Eggs
- bell peppers
- taters
- Sprouts
- The onion
- Salt
- Chili

Nutritional value:

Low carb, high protein, high in C and A vitamins.

Recipes substitute:
For variation, try adding some asparagus or mushrooms.

Preparation methods:

1. In a bowl, whisk the eggs.
2. Chop the onion, spinach, tomatoes, and bell peppers.
3. In a skillet, sauté chopped veggies.
4. Over the sautéed vegetables, pour whisked eggs.
5. Cook the omelette until it sets.

Wrap with avocadoe and vegetables

Cooking time: 5 minutes   **Portion size:** 1 wrap

Ingredients:

- Whole-grain tortilla
- Avocado
- cured salmon
- cucumber

Nutritional value:

Fiber, omega-3 fatty acids, and healthy fats.

Recipes substitute:
In place of the salmon, use tofu or turkey.

Preparation methods:

1. Mozzarella should be spread over the whole-grain wrap.
2. Top with smoked salmon.
3. Lay slices of cucumber on top of the salmon.
4. The wrap should be rolled up.

Greek Yogurt Parfait

Cooking time: 5 minutes   **Portion size:** 1 parfait.

Ingredients:

- Greek yogurt
- Berries
- Nuts
- Chia seeds

Nutritional value:

plenty of antioxidants, probiotics, and protein.

Recipes substitute:

Swap out the fruits or granola.

Preparation methods:

1. Scoop Greek yogurt into a glass's bottom layer.
2. Spread some berries on top.
3. Add chia seeds and nuts.
4. Iterate through the levels.

Pudding
with Chia Seeds

Cooking time: There is no need to cook.   **Portion size:** 1 portion..

Ingredients:
- Chia seeds
- Almond milk
- extract from vanilla
- Berries.

Nutritional value:

High in fiber and omega-3 fatty acids.

Recipes substitute:

Preparation methods:
1. In a bowl, combine almond milk, vanilla, and chia seeds.
2. Keep the mixture chilled for the entire night.
3. Drizzle with berries to serve.

Breakfast Bowl with Quinoa

Cooking time: 15 minutes.

Portion size: One Bowl.

Ingredients:

- Quinoa
- Almond milk
- Slices of banana
- Nuts (almonds or walnuts)
- Turnip

Nutritional value:

Rich in potassium, fiber, and protein.

Recipes substitute:

You can also use berries or, if you'd like, a drizzle of honey.

Preparation methods:

1. Prepare the quinoa with almond milk, following the directions on the package.
2. Add almonds and banana slices on top.
3. Add a dash of cinnamon.

Egg Muffins with Feta

Cooking time: 20 minutes   **Portion size:** 2 egg muffins

Ingredients:

- Eggs
- Sprouts
- Feta cheese
- Salt
- Chili

Nutritional value:

Rich in protein and abundant in vitamins A and B

Recipes substitute:

To provide more flavor, add diced tomatoes or mushrooms.

Preparation methods:

1. Set the oven's temperature to 175°C/350°F.
2. Add salt and pepper to the eggs as you whisk them.
3. Add the crumbled feta and chopped spinach and stir.
4. Fill muffin cups with mixture.
5. Bake until the eggs are set, about 20 minutes.

Almond Pancakes with Flour and Spinach

Cooking time: 10 minutes   **Portion size:** 3 pancakes.

Ingredients:
- Almond meal
- Eggs
- Almond milk
- powdered baking
- extract from vanilla

Nutritional value:
Rich in protein, devoid of gluten and carbs.

Recipes substitute:
You can also use coconut flour or sugar with blueberries.

Preparation methods:
1. Combine almond flour, baking powder, almond milk, eggs, and vanilla.
2. Transfer the batter to a heated griddle.
3. Stir and continue cooking until bubbles appear on one side of the food.

Toast with mashed avocado and poached eggs

Cooking time: 15 minutes   **Portion size:** 1 or 2 toast slices

Ingredients:

- Bread made with whole grains
- Avocado
- Eggs
- Salt
- Chili

Nutritional value:

Fiber, protein, and healthy fats.

Recipes substitute:

Use sourdough or multigrain bread

Preparation methods:

1. Toast pieces of wholegrain bread.
2. Over the toast, mash the ripe avocado.
3. Add poached eggs on top.
4. Add pepper and salt for seasoning.

Chia Seed Pudding with Coconut

Cooking time: There is no need to cook   **Portion size:** 1 portion.

Ingredients:
- Chia seeds
- Milk from coconuts
- extract from vanilla
- coconut shreds

Nutritional value:

High in fiber and good fats.

Recipes substitute:

To add a tropical flair, add mango or pineapple.

Preparation methods:
1. Combine the vanilla, coconut milk, and chia seeds.
2. Store in the fridge all night.
3. Before serving, sprinkle shredded coconut on top.

Turkey and Veggie Skillet

Cooking time: 15 minutes.　　　　**Portion size:** 1 skillet.

Ingredients:
- Turkey on the ground
- bell peppers
- Zucchini
- The onion
- Eggs
- Salt
- Chili

Nutritional value:
Vitamins, low carbs, and high protein.

Recipes substitute:
In place of the turkey, use lean chicken or tofu.

Preparation methods:
1. Melt turkey meat in a skillet.
2. When the veggies are soft, add them diced and sauté.
3. Once eggs are cracked into the skillet, fry them to the desired doneness

Almond and Blueberry Overnight Oats

Cooking time: There is no need to cook.   **Portion size:** 1 portion.

Ingredients:
- Oats rolled
- Almond milk
- berries
- Slices of almonds
- Chia seeds

Nutritional value:
Antioxidants, fiber, and good fats

Recipes substitute:
Alternate berries or top with a dollop of yogurt

Preparation methods:
1. In a jar, combine oats, almond milk, chia seeds, blueberries, and almond slices.
2. Store in the fridge all night.
3. Before serving, stir.

Kale
and Sweet Potato Hash

Cooking time: 20 minutes   **Portion size:** 1 portion.

Ingredients:

- yams
- Kale
- The onion
- Olive oil
- Paprika
- Powdered garlic

Nutritional value:

High in fiber and vitamins A and C, this food is nutritious.

Recipes substitute:

Replace sweet potatoes with butternut squash

Preparation methods:

1. Sweet potatoes should be diced and cooked in olive oil until soft.
2. Add the chopped onion and kale, and heat until the kale wilts.
3. Add garlic powder and paprika for seasoning.

Coconut Chia Popsicles with Raspberry

Cooking time: There is no need to cook.   **Portion size:** 1 popsicle

Ingredients:
- Berries
- Water from coconuts
- Chia seeds

Nutritional value:

fiber, antioxidants, and hydration.

Recipes substitute:

Try different berries or squeeze in some lime juice.

Preparation methods:
1. Blend coconut water and raspberries.
2. Add the chia seeds and stir.
3. Fill popsicle molds, then freeze.

Breakfast bowl with broccoli and cauliflower

Cooking time: 15 minutes   **Portion size:** 1 Bowl.

Ingredients:

- Rice made from cauliflower
- Broccoli
- Rosy tomatoes
- Poached egg
- Olive oil
- Salt

Nutritional value:

Rich in vitamins, low in carbohydrates.

Recipes substitute:

Use green beans or asparagus

Preparation methods:

1. Broccoli and cauliflower rice are sautéed in olive oil.
2. Include cherry tomatoes.
3. Add a poached egg on top and sprinkle with salt.

Bowl of Mango and Mint Smoothie

Cooking time: 5 minutes

Portion size: 1 Bowl.

Ingredients:

- pieces of frozen mango
- Greek yogurt
- Almond milk
- mint leaves that are fresh
- Chia seeds

Nutritional value:

Rich in omega-3 fatty acids, probiotics, and vitamin C.

Recipes substitute:

To add more nutrients, use pineapple or add spinach.

Preparation methods:

1. Mango, Greek yogurt, and almond milk should be blended until smooth.
2. Transfer into a bowl and garnish with chia seeds and mint leaves.

Breakfast Casserole with Turkey and Spinach

Cooking time: 30 minutes   **Portion size:** 1 Bowl.

Ingredients:
- Turkey on the ground
- Sprouts
- Eggs
- Almond milk
- The onion
- Garlic
- Salt
- Chili

Nutritional value:
Rich in vitamins, iron, and protein.

Recipes substitute:
For variation, try using ground chicken or adding bell peppers.

Preparation methods:
1. Add onions and garlic to brown ground turkey.
2. Whisk eggs, almond milk, pepper, and salt in a bowl.
3. Stir in spinach and sautéed turkey, then transfer to a baking dish.
4. Bake until solidified.

Frittata with zucchini and tomatoes

Cooking time: 25 minutes   **Portion size:** 1 Frittata.

Ingredients:

- Zucchini
- taters
- Eggs
- Cheese Parmesan
- Olive oil
- Basil

Nutritional value:

Vitamins A and K, protein, and nutrition value.

Recipes substitute:

feta cheese or extra greens like spinach.

Preparation methods:

1. Sliced zucchini should be sautéed in olive oil until tender.
2. Stir in the chopped tomatoes and heat through.
3. Pour eggs over veggies after whisking in Parmesan cheese.
4. After baking until firm, top with freshly chopped basil.

Banana and peanut butter smoothie

Cooking time: 5 minutes   **Portion size:** 1 Smoothie.

Ingredients:
- Banana
- Almond butter
- Almond milk
- Greek yogurt
- Cubes of ice

Nutritional value:

Healthy fats, potassium, and protein.

Recipes substitute:

Add a handful of spinach or another type of nut butter.

Preparation methods:
1. Greek yogurt, peanut butter, banana, and almond milk should all be blended until smooth.
2. Mix with the ice cubes once more.

Cinnamon Apple Chia Pudding

Cooking time: There is no need to cook.   **Portion size:** 1 portion.

Ingredients:
- Eggs
- broccoli
- Cheese cheddar
- Milk
- Salt
- Chili

Nutritional value:

Vitamins and fiber.

Recipes substitute:

Add a handful of spinach or another type of nut butter.

Preparation methods:
1. Broccoli should be steamed until soft.
2. Beat eggs with milk, pepper, and salt.
3. Add chopped broccoli to shredded cheddar cheese.
4. Transfer the egg mixture into muffin tins, then top with cheese and broccoli.
5. Eggs should be baked until set.

Cinnamon Apple Chia Pudding and Broccoli

Cooking time: There is no need to cook.   **Portion size:** 1 portion.

Ingredients:
- Chia seeds
- Almond milk
- sliced apples
- Turnip
- (Optional) maple syrup

Nutritional value:
Protein and calcium

Recipes substitute:
Change up the fruit or mix in a dash of nutmeg.

Preparation methods:
1. Combine almond milk, maple syrup, cinnamon, and chia seeds.
2. Put in the fridge until it becomes the consistency of pudding.
3. Before serving, place some apple slices on top.

Lunchtime Recipes

Nourishing and Satisfying Lunch Recipes.

Salad with Grilled Chicken

Cooking time: 15 minutes   **Portion size:** 1 portion.

Ingredients:

- Breast of chicken
- mixed greens for salad
- rosy tomatoes
- cucumber
- Onion red
- Olive oil
- Juice from lemons
- Salt
- Chili

Nutritional value:

High in fiber, vitamins, and protein, making it a nutritious food.

Recipes substitute:

To make it creamier, add avocado or use turkey in place of the chicken.

Preparation methods:

1. Use salt and pepper to season the chicken.
2. Cook on the grill until done.
3. Combine red onion, cucumber, cherry tomatoes, and salad leaves.
4. Place sliced grilled chicken on top.
5. Pour in some lemon juice and olive oil.

Pesto-Garlic Zucchini Noodles

Cooking time: 10 minutes   **Portion size:** 1 portion.

Ingredients:
- Zucchini
- rosy tomatoes
- Pesto pasta
- Cheese Parmesan
- Pine Nuts

Nutritional value:
Vitamins, good fats, and low carbs

Recipes substitute:
You can also add grilled prawns or use spiralized sweet potatoes

Preparation methods:
1. Stir-fry the zucchini to make noodles.
2. Noodles of zucchini are sautéed till soft.
3. Toss with pesto sauce and cherry tomatoes.
4. Sprinkle pine nuts and Parmesan cheese over top.

Soup with Lentils and Veggies

Cooking time: 30 minutes   **Portion size:** 1 bowl.

Ingredients:
- lentils
- Carapace
- Celery
- The onion
- Garlic
- Broth made of vegetables
- Bay leaves
- Combine
- Coriander
- Salt
- Chili

Nutritional value:

High in vitamins, protein, and fiber, making it a nutritious food.

Recipes substitute:

To provide more greens, add spinach or kale.

Preparation methods:

1. Stir-fry the zucchini to make noodles.
2. Noodles of zucchini are sautéed till soft.
3. ToCarrots, celery, onion, and garlic are sautéed.
4. Add the lentils, coriander, cumin, bay leaves, salt, and pepper.
5. Once the lentils are soft, simmer them.ss with pesto sauce and cherry tomatoes.
6. Sprinkle pine nuts and Parmesan cheese over top.

Packets of salmon and asparagus in foil

Cooking time: 20 minutes

Portion size: 1 packet.

Ingredients:
- Fillet of salmon
- spears of asparagus
- Slices of lemon
- Garlic
- Dill
- Olive oil
- Salt
- Chili

Nutritional value:
Omega-3 fatty acids, vitamins, and antioxidants

Recipes substitute:
In place of salmon, use cod or tilapia.

Preparation methods:
1. Lay the salmon fillet onto a piece of foil.
2. Place the asparagus next to the fish.
3. Add the lemon slices, olive oil, salt, pepper, minced garlic, and dill.
4. Place inside a package and cook.

Bell peppers filled with spinach and chickpeas

Cooking time: 25 minutes   **Portion size:** 1 pepper.

Ingredients:

- bell peppers
- garbanzo beans
- Sprouts
- taters
- Onion red
- Garlic
- Combine
- Paprika
- Salt
- Chili

Nutritional value:

Vitamins, fiber, and protein

Recipes substitute:

Try quinoa in place of the chickpeas.

Preparation methods:

1. Remove the seeds after halves the bell peppers.
2. Add the garlic, red onion, tomatoes, spinach, and chickpeas and sauté.
3. Add salt, pepper, paprika, and cumin for seasoning.
4. After packing the mixture inside bell peppers, bake them.

Lettuce Wraps with Turkey

Cooking time: 15 minutes   **Portion size:** 2 or 3 wraps.

Ingredients:

- Turkey on the ground
- Iceberg or butter lettuce leaves
- bell peppers
- Carapace
- Green onions
- Soy sauce
- Ginger
- Garlic
- oil from sesame

Nutritional value:

Vitamins, low carbs, and lean protein

Recipes substitute:

For a vegetarian version, use tofu or ground chicken.

Preparation methods:

1. In a pan, brown the ground turkey.
2. Add the garlic, ginger, green onions, shredded carrots, and sliced bell peppers.
3. Add sesame oil and soy sauce and stir.
4. Spoon mixture into leaves of lettuce.

Stacks of eggplant and tomatoes

Cooking time: 20 minutes

Portion size: 1 portion.

Ingredients:

- eggplant
- taters
- Cheese mozzarella
- fresh basil
- Olive oil
- vinegar with balsamic
- Salt
- Chili

Nutritional value:

Calcium, antioxidants, and fiber.

Recipes substitute:

Mash red peppers or use goat cheese.

Preparation methods:

1. Cut tomatoes and eggplant into slices.
2. Add fresh mozzarella slices and basil leaves to the layer.
3. Drizzle with balsamic vinegar and olive oil.
4. Add a dash of pepper and salt.

Stuffed peppers with black beans and quinoa

Cooking time: 25 minutes

Portion size: 1 portion.

Ingredients:

- bell peppers
- Quinoa
- Dark beans
- corn
- Salsa
- Combine
- powdered chilies
- Powdered garlic
- Onion

Nutritional value:

Vitamins, fiber, and protein

Recipes substitute:

In place of the quinoa, use brown rice.

Preparation methods:

1. Follow the directions on the package to cook the quinoa.
2. Add chopped cilantro, cumin, chili powder, garlic powder, black beans, corn, and salsa to the quinoa.
3. After packing the mixture inside bell peppers, bake them.

Avocado and Tuna Lettuce Cups

Cooking time: 10 minutes   **Portion size:** 2 or 3 portion size.

Ingredients:
- Tuna canned
- Avocado
- Celery
- Onion red
- Juice from lemons
- Dill
- Salt
- Chili

Nutritional value:

Omega-3 fatty acids, protein, and vitamins make up nutritional value.

Recipes substitute:

In place of the tuna, use cooked chicken or shrimp.

Preparation methods:

1. After draining the canned tuna, combine it with diced avocado, red onion, celery, lemon juice, and dill.
2. Add pepper and salt for seasoning.
3. Transfer to lettuce cups.

Fried cauliflower rice

Cooking time: 15 minutes

Portion size: 1 portion.

Ingredients:
- rice made from cauliflower
- Prawns
- Peas
- Carapace
- Eggs
- Soy sauce
- oil from sesame
- Green onions

Nutritional value:
Low carb, high protein.

Recipes substitute:
In place of the shrimp, use chicken or tofu.

Preparation methods:
1. In a pan, sauté the shrimp, peas, and carrots.
2. Place ingredients aside and use the empty area to scramble eggs.
3. Stir in sesame oil, soy sauce, and cauliflower rice.
4. Add chopped green onions as a garnish.

Grilled chicken over a Greek salad

Cooking time: 15 minutes   **Portion size:** 1 portion.

Ingredients:

- Breast of chicken
- Lettuce Romaine
- cucumber
- rosy tomatoes
- Onion red
- Olives kalamata
- Feta cheese
- Olive oil
- Vinegar of red wine
- Oregano, dried
- Salt

Nutritional value:

Healthful fats, fiber, vitamins, and protein.

Recipes substitute:

As an alternative to chicken, try grilled tofu or chickpeas.

Preparation methods:

1. After the chicken is thoroughly cooked, slice it.
2. Dice the tomatoes, red onion, cucumber, and romaine lettuce.
3. Add feta cheese crumbles and olives.
4. Add a drizzle of red wine vinegar, olive oil, oregano, salt, and pepper.
5. Add slices of cooked chicken on top.

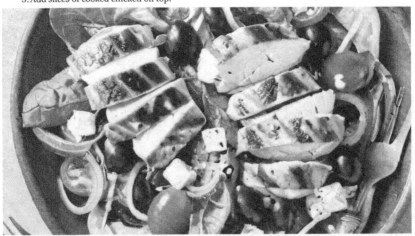

Salad Caprese with Balsamic Vinegar

Cooking time: 10 minutes

Portion size: 1 portion.

Ingredients:

- recent mozzarella cheese
- taters
- fresh leaves of basil
- Balsamic reduction
- Olive oil
- Salt
- Chili

Nutritional value:

Antioxidants, calcium, and good fats.

Recipes substitute:

For an alternative presentation, consider using cherry tomatoes and tiny mozzarella balls as replacements.

Preparation methods:

1. Cut tomatoes and mozzarella cheese into slices.
2. Add a layer of recent basil leaves.
3. Drizzle with olive oil and balsamic glaze.
4. To taste, add salt and pepper for seasoning.

Stir-fried Tofu with Vegetables

Cooking time: 20 minutes   **Portion size:** 1 portion.

Ingredients:

- Added firm tofu
- broccoli
- bell peppers
- Snap peas
- Carapace
- Soy sauce
- Garlic
- Ginger
- oil from sesame
- Flakes of red pepper
- Green onions

Nutritional value:

Vitamins, fiber, and protein.

Recipes substitute:

In place of tofu, use seitan or tempeh.

Preparation methods:

1. Tofu should be pressed to remove extra moisture and cube.
2. Sesame oil is used to sauté tofu till golden brown.
3. Add the ginger, garlic, and chopped veggies.
4. Add the red pepper flakes and soy sauce and stir.
5. Add sliced green onions as a garnish.

Quiche with spinach and mushrooms

Cooking time: 45 minutes

Portion size: 1 slice is the portion size.

Ingredients:

- Pie crust (homemade or from the shop)
- Eggs
- Sprouts
- fungi
- The onion
- Garlic
- Milk
- Swiss cheese
- Salt
- Chili
- Ginger

Nutritional value:

Vitamins, calcium, and protein

Recipes substitute:

Replace the Swiss cheese with feta or cheddar.

Preparation methods:

1. Bake pie crust blind while preheating the oven.
2. Garlic, onion, mushrooms, and spinach should be sautéed until wilted.
3. Beat eggs with milk, nutmeg, salt, and pepper.
4. In the pie crust, arrange the spinach mixture and Swiss cheese.
5. Cover the filling with the egg mixture.
6. Bake until golden brown and set.

Avocado
and Cucumber Rolls

Cooking time: 30 minutes   **Portion size:** 1 serving (about 6-8 pieces).

Ingredients:

- sushi rice
- Sheets of nori seaweed
- cucumber
- Avocado
- vinegar made from rice
- Soy sauce
- Wasabi
- pickled ginger

Nutritional value:

For added taste, try adding crab or smoked salmon.

Recipes substitute:

Vitamins, fiber, and good fats.

Preparation methods:

1. Prepare sushi rice as directed on the bag, adding a dash of rice vinegar for seasoning.
2. Lay a sheet of nori on a sushi mat made of bamboo.
3. Leaving a border, cover the nori with a layer of rice.
4. Add the avocado and cucumber strips.
5. Roll tightly with the mat made of bamboo.
6. Cut into sushi rolls and present with pickled ginger, wasabi, and soy sauce.

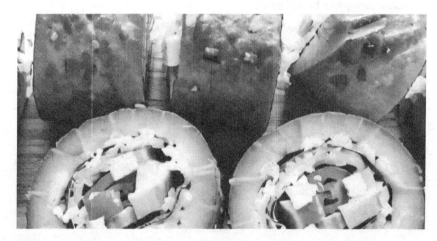

Bowl of sweet potatoes with black beans

Cooking time: 30 minutes

Portion size: 1 bowl.

Ingredients:

- Yams
- Dark beans
- corn
- Avocado
- Lime juice
- Onion
- Combine
- Paprika
- Salt
- Chili

Nutritional value:

Vitamins, Protein, and Fiber.

Recipes substitute:

Add cherry tomatoes or quinoa in place of the sweet potatoes.

Preparation methods:

1. Sweet potatoes should be roasted until they are soft.
2. Combine corn, sliced avocado, black beans, chopped cilantro, lime juice, paprika, cumin, and salt & pepper.
3. Top with the roasted sweet potatoes and serve.

Skewers of chicken and vegetables

Cooking time: 20 minutes   **Portion size:** 1 portion.

Ingredients:

- Breast of chicken
- Bell peppers (many hues)
- rosy tomatoes
- Zucchini
- Olive oil
- Garlic
- Oregano
- Juice from lemons
- Salt
- Chili

Nutritional value:

Antioxidants, vitamins, and protein.

Recipes substitute:

In place of the chicken, use tofu or shrimp.

Preparation methods:

1. Cube the chicken and marinate it in a mixture of olive oil, lemon juice, oregano, minced garlic, salt, and pepper.
2. Put veggies and chicken on skewers.
3. Cook the chicken on the grill until it's done.

Drop Soup with Eggs

Cooking time: 10 minutes

Portion size: 1 bowl.

Ingredients:

- Broth made with vegetables or chicken
- Eggs
- Green onions
- Ginger
- Soy sauce
- oil from sesame

Nutritional value:

Vitamins and protein

Recipes substitute:

Tofu or spinach can be used to add more texture.

Preparation methods:

1. Simmer the broth with the ginger slices.
2. Whisk together the beaten eggs and gradually add them to the boiling broth.
3. Add sesame oil and soy sauce for seasoning.
4. Add chopped green onions as a garnish.

Stir-fried Turkey with Cabbage

Cooking time: 20 minutes   **Portion size:** 1 portion.

Ingredients:

- Turkey on the ground
- Broccoli
- Carapace
- Peas in the snow
- Garlic
- Ginger
- Soy sauce
- oil from sesame
- Green onions

Nutritional value:

Vitamins, fiber, and protein

Recipes substitute:

Use ground beef or chicken

Preparation methods:

1. In a pan, brown the ground turkey.
2. Add the ginger, minced garlic, julienned carrots, snow peas, and shredded cabbage.
3. Add sesame oil and soy sauce and stir.
4. Add sliced green onions as a garnish.

Avocado
And shrimp salad

Cooking time: 15 minutes

Portion size: 1 portion.

Ingredients:

- Prawns
- Avocado
- Various greens
- rosy tomatoes
- Onion red
- Onion
- Lime juice
- Olive oil
- Salt
- Chili

Nutritional value:

Vitamins, good fats, and protein

Recipes substitute:

Use tofu or grilled chicken

Preparation methods:

1. Cook shrimp by sautéing them.
2. Combine chopped red onion, chopped cilantro, halved cherry tomatoes, cubed avocado, and mixed greens.
3. Olive oil and lime juice should be drizzled on.
4. Add cooked shrimp on top.

Dinner Delights

Flavourful Dinner Recipes

Baked Chicken with Lemon Herbs

Cooking time: 35 minutes

Portion size: 2 thighs.

Ingredients:

- Thighs of chicken
- Lemon
- pristine rosemary
- New thyme
- Garlic
- Olive oil
- Salt
- Chili

Nutritional value:

Healthful fats, vitamins, and protein.

Recipes substitute:

Drumsticks or chicken breasts

Preparation methods:

1. Set the oven to preheat.
2. Chicken thighs should be rubbed with olive oil, lemon juice, minced garlic, chopped rosemary, chopped thyme, and salt and pepper.
3. Bake the chicken until it's cooked through and golden.

Pizza with Cauliflower Crust

Cooking time: 30 minutes   **Portion size:** 1 or 2 slices each portion.

Ingredients:

- Lettuce
- Eggs
- Cheese mozzarella
- tomato sauce (devoid of sugar)
- Basil
- rosy tomatoes
- Olive oil
- Salt
- Chili

Nutritional value:

Low in carbohydrates, rich in vitamins and antioxidants.

Recipes substitute:

You can use store-bought crust or almond flour.

Preparation methods:

1. microwave and rice cauliflower.
2. To make a dough, combine with the eggs, mozzarella, and seasonings.
3. Shape into a crust, then bake for golden brown.
4. Add cherry tomatoes, basil, olive oil, salt, and pepper on top.

Salmon on the Grill with Asparagus

Cooking time: 15 minutes

Portion size: 1 fillet.

Ingredients:

- Filets of salmon
- Asparagus
- Lemon
- Dill
- Olive oil
- Garlic
- Salt
- Chili

Nutritional value:

Fiber, vitamins, and omega-3 fatty acids.

Recipes substitute:

Replace with trout or cod.

Preparation methods:

1. Lemon juice, dill, olive oil, minced garlic, salt, and pepper are used to season salmon.
2. Cook the asparagus and fish on the grill.
3. Before serving, squeeze some fresh lemon over the top.

Cherry tomatoes and pesto-crusted zoodles

Cooking time: 10 minutes

Portion size: 1 portion.

Ingredients:
- Zucchini
- Pesto pasta
- rosy tomatoes
- Pine Nuts
- Cheese Parmesan

Nutritional value:

Vitamins, good fats, low carbs.

Recipes substitute:

Squash with spaghetti squash in place of zoodles.

Preparation methods:
1. Stir-fry the zucchini to make noodles.
2. Zoodles should be sautéed until they are somewhat soft.
3. Add toasted pine nuts, Parmesan cheese, halved cherry tomatoes, and pesto sauce.

Stir-fried turkey with vegetables

Cooking time: 20 minutes   **Portion size:** 1 portion.

Ingredients:

- Turkey on the ground
- broccoli
- bell peppers
- Snap peas
- Carapace
- Garlic
- Ginger
- Soy sauce
- oil from sesame
- Green onions

Preparation methods:

Nutritional value:

Vitamins, fiber, and protein

Recipes substitute:

In place of the turkey, use tofu or chicken.

1. In a pan, brown the ground turkey.
2. Add the ginger, bell peppers, snap peas, chopped broccoli, and minced garlic.
3. Add sesame oil and soy sauce and stir.
4. Add sliced green onions as a garnish.

Stir-fried shrimp and broccoli

Cooking time: 15 minutes   **Portion size:** 1 portion.

Ingredients:

- Prawns
- florets of broccoli
- Bell peppers in red
- Garlic
- Ginger
- Soy sauce
- oil from sesame
- Olive oil
- Green onions

Nutritional value:

Vitamins, fiber, and protein

Recipes substitute:

In place of the shrimp, use chicken or tofu.

Preparation methods:

1. Sauté shrimp in olive oil until pink.
2. Add broccoli, sliced red bell pepper, minced garlic, and ginger.
3. Stir in soy sauce and sesame oil.
4. Garnish with chopped green onions.

Pasta Squash with Basil and Tomato

Cooking time: 40 minutes

Portion size: 1 portion.

Ingredients:
- A spaghetti squash
- taters
- fresh basil
- Garlic
- Olive oil
- Salt
- Chili
- Flakes of red pepper (optional)

Nutritional value:

Low in carbohydrates, rich in vitamins and antioxidants.

Recipes substitute:

If preferred, use whole-grain pasta.

Preparation methods:
1. Roast the spaghetti squash until it's easy to peel the threads off.
2. In olive oil, sauté diced tomatoes, minced garlic, and finely chopped fresh basil.
3. Combine the tomato mixture with the squash.
4. If preferred, add red pepper flakes, salt, and pepper for seasoning.

Skewers of grilled vegetables

Cooking time: 20 minutes   **Portion size:** 1 portion.

Ingredients:

- Rosy tomatoes
- Zucchini
- fungi
- Onion red
- Bell peppers (many hues)
- Olive oil
- vinegar with balsamic
- Garlic
- Rosemary
- Salt
- Chili

Nutritional value:

Antioxidants and vitamins.

Recipes substitute:

For more protein, add halloumi or tofu.

Preparation methods:

1. Cherry tomatoes, bell peppers, mushrooms, zucchini pieces, and red onions should all be threaded onto skewers.
2. Combine olive oil, balsamic vinegar, chopped rosemary, minced garlic, salt, and pepper.
3. After brushing the skewers with the mixture, broil the vegetables until they are soft.

Bell peppers stuffed with quinoa

Cooking time: 25 minutes

Portion size: 1 pepper.

Ingredients:

- bell peppers
- Quinoa
- Dark beans
- corn
- Salsa
- Combine
- powdered chilies
- Powdered garlic
- Onion
- Lime juice
- (Optional) avocado

Nutritional value:

Vitamins, fiber, and protein.

Recipes substitute:

In place of the quinoa, use brown rice.

Preparation methods:

1. Follow the directions on the package to cook the quinoa.
2. Add cooked quinoa to chopped cilantro, lime juice, black beans, corn, salsa, cumin, and chili and garlic powders.
3. Stuff the quinoa mixture inside bell peppers.
4. Bake peppers until they become soft.
5. If preferred, top with sliced avocado and serve.

Served with Mediterranean Salsa, Baked Cod

Cooking time: 20 minutes   **Portion size:** 1 fillet.

Ingredients:

- Fillets of cod
- rosy tomatoes
- Olives kalamata
- Onion red
- cucumber
- Feta cheese
- Olive oil
- Juice from lemons
- Oregano
- Salt
- Chili

Nutritional value:

Omega-3 fatty acids, protein, and vitamins.

Recipes substitute:

Use sea bass or halibut

Preparation methods:

1. Set the oven to preheat.
2. Cod fillets are seasoned with salt, pepper, oregano, lemon juice, and olive oil.
3. Fish should flake readily after baking.
4. In the meantime, make the salsa by adding some diced cherry tomatoes, red onion, cucumber, feta cheese, and olive oil.
5. Before serving, spoon salsa over the baked cod.

Lasagna with eggplant

Cooking time: 45 minutes   **Portion size:** 1 portion.

Ingredients:
- Turkey on the ground
- tomato sauce (devoid of sugar)
- Cheese mozzarella
- Cheese ricotta
- Cheese Parmesan
- Garlic
- Basil
- Oregano
- Salt
- Chili

Nutritional value:

Vitamins, fiber, and protein

Recipes substitute:

Use ground beef or plant-based meat.

Preparation methods:
1. Set the oven to preheat.
2. Once the eggplant is thinly sliced, broil it until it becomes soft.
3. Brown ground turkey in a pan with minced garlic, oregano, basil, and salt & pepper.
4. Arrange the grilled eggplant, turkey mixture, tomato sauce, mozzarella, and ricotta cheese in a baking dish.
5. Layer again, then sprinkle Parmesan on top.
6. Bake till golden and bubbling.

Wraps with avocado and chicken salad

Cooking time: 15 minutes   **Portion size:** 2 or 3 wraps.

Ingredients:
- Breast of chicken
- Avocado
- Greek yogurt
- Lime juice
- Onion
- Lettuce stems
- rosy tomatoes
- Onion red
- Salt
- Chili

Nutritional value:

Vitamins, good fats, and protein

Recipes substitute:

Try tofu or turkey for variation.

Preparation methods:

1. Cook the chicken completely on the grill.
2. Avocado should be mashed and combined with Greek yogurt, chopped cilantro, lime juice, salt, and pepper.
3. Distribute the avocado blend among the lettuce leaves.
4. Add chopped red onion, cherry tomatoes, and cooked chicken on top.
5. Form into wraps.

Inflatable Acorn Squash

Cooking time: 40 minutes

Portion size: 1/2 squash.

Ingredients:
- Acorn squash
- Quinoa
- garbanzo beans
- Sprouts
- Bell peppers in red
- The onion
- Garlic
- Combine
- Paprika
- Olive oil
- Salt
- Chili

Nutritional value:

Vitamins, fiber, and protein

Recipes substitute:

In place of acorn squash, use sweet potatoes.

Preparation methods:

1. Acorn squash should be cut in half and roasted until soft.
2. Cook quinoa and add cumin, paprika, salt, and pepper to a sauté pan along with chickpeas, spinach, diced red bell pepper, onion, and garlic.
3. Spoon the quinoa mixture into each side of the squash.
4. After drizzling with olive oil, bake until well warm.

Soup with vegetables and turkey

Cooking time: 30 minutes   **Portion size:** 1 bowl.

Ingredients:
- Turkey on the ground
- Carapace
- Celery
- The onion
- Garlic
- broccoli
- Lettuce
- Broth made from chicken.
- thyme
- Rosemary
- Salt
- Chili

Nutritional value:
Vitamins, fiber, and protein

Recipes substitute:
Use ground beef or chicken

Preparation methods:
1. In a saucepan, brown ground turkey.
2. Add the diced carrots, onion, celery, minced garlic, broccoli, cauliflower, rosemary, thyme, and salt and pepper to taste.
3. After adding the chicken broth, boil the vegetables until they are soft.

Stuffed Portobello Mushrooms with Quinoa

Cooking time: 35 minutes

Portion size: 1 or 2 mushrooms.

Ingredients:

- Portobello fungi
- Quinoa
- Sprouts
- Bell peppers in red
- The onion
- Garlic
- Broth made of vegetables
- Cheese Parmesan
- Olive oil
- Salt
- Chili

Nutritional value:

Vitamins, fiber, and protein

Recipes substitute:

In place of quinoa, use couscous.

Preparation methods:

1. Set the oven to preheat.
2. Clean the portobello mushrooms after removing the stems.
3. Prepare quinoa in vegetable broth as directed on the package.
4. Garlic, onion, red bell pepper, and chopped spinach should all be sautéed until tender.
5. Add Parmesan cheese and sautéed veggies to cooked quinoa.
6. Stuff the quinoa mixture inside the mushrooms.
7. Add a drizzle of olive oil and season with pepper and salt.
8. Bake the mushrooms until they become soft.

Brown rice stir-fried with tofu and vegetables

Cooking time: 30 minutes   **Portion size:** 1 portion.

Ingredients:

- Sturdy tofu
- broccoli
- Snap peas
- Carapace
- bell peppers
- The onion
- Garlic
- Soy sauce
- vinegar made from rice
- oil from sesame
- Grains of brown rice
- Green onions

Nutritional value:

Vitamins, fiber, and protein.

Recipes substitute:

Use quinoa in place of brown rice or tempeh in place of tofu.

Preparation methods:

1. Cut tofu into cubes after pressing to eliminate excess moisture.
2. Once tofu is golden brown, stir-fry it and set it aside.
3. Broccoli slices, snap peas, carrots, onion, bell peppers, and minced garlic are sautéed.
4. Return the cooked tofu to the pan and mix in the sesame oil, rice vinegar, and soy sauce.
5. Add some sliced green onions as a garnish and serve over cooked brown rice.

Mediterranean Salad with Chickpeas

Cooking time: 15 minutes, including prep.   **Portion size:** 1 portion.

Ingredients:

- garbanzo beans
- cucumber
- rosy tomatoes
- Onion red
- Olives kalamata
- Feta cheese
- Olive oil
- Juice from lemons
- Garlic
- Oregano
- Salt
- Chili

Nutritional value:

Vitamins, fiber, and protein.

Recipes substitute:

Swap out the chickpeas for couscous or quinoa.

Preparation methods:

1. Empty and rinse the chickpeas.
2. Dice cucumber, pit olives, halve cherry tomatoes, and slice red onion.
3. Mix the veggies, feta cheese crumbles, minced garlic, olive oil, lemon juice, oregano, salt, and pepper with the chickpeas.
4. Toss until thoroughly mixed.

Green Bean Almondine

Cooking time: 15 minutes   **Portion size:** 1 cup.

Ingredients:

- Green beans
- Almonds
- Lemon zest
- Olive oil
- Garlic
- Salt
- Pepper

Nutritional value:

Low in calories, vitamin A & C

Recipes substitute:

Vegetables like asparagus or broccoli.

Preparation methods:

1. Bring a pot of water to a boil and blanch the green beans for about 2-3 minutes, until they are bright green and crisp-tender.
2. Drain the green beans and immediately plunge them into a bowl of ice water to stop the cooking process. Drain again and set aside.
3. Heat a skillet over medium heat and add slivered almonds. Toast the almonds, stirring frequently, until they are golden and fragrant.
4. Add minced garlic to the skillet and sauté for about 1 minute, until fragrant.
5. Toss in the blanched green beans and cook for another 2-3 minutes, until heated through.
6. Remove the skillet from heat and stir in lemon zest, a drizzle of olive oil, salt, and pepper.
7. Transfer the green beans to a serving dish and garnish with additional lemon zest and almonds.

Packets of vegetable and salmon foil

Cooking time: 20 minutes

Portion size: 1 packet.

Ingredients:
- Filets of salmon
- Asparagus
- rosy tomatoes
- Zucchini
- Bell peppers in red
- Lemon
- Olive oil
- Garlic
- Dill
- Salt
- Chili

Nutritional value:

Omega-3 fatty acids, vitamins, and antioxidants

Recipes substitute:

If salmon isn't available, use cod or trout.

Preparation methods:
1. Set the oven to preheat.
2. Line a piece of foil with each salmon fillet.
3. Put the veggies in a circle around the salmon.
4. Add a drizzle of olive oil, lemon juice, minced garlic, dill, salt, and pepper.
5. Place the salmon inside the sealed packages and bake until it's done.

Curry with Lentils and Veggies

Cooking time: 35 minutes   **Portion size:** 1 portion.

Ingredients:

- one cup of lentils, dried
- one sliced onion
- two minced garlic cloves
- One tablespoon of freshly grated ginger
- two diced bell peppers
- two sliced carrots
- 1 cup of florets of cauliflower
- One 14-oz can of coconut milk
- Two tablespoons tomato paste
- One spoonful of curry powder
- One tsp of turmeric
- One teaspoon of cumin
- One tsp of coriander
- Two tsp olive oil
- To taste, add salt and pepper.

Nutritional value:

Protein: One excellent source of plant-based protein is lentils.
Fiber: Vegetables and lentils add to the amount of fiber in the diet.
Vitamins: Carrots and bell peppers are good sources of vitamins A and C.
Good Fats: Olive oil and coconut milk both contain good fats.

Recipes substitute:

Replace the lentils with kidney beans or chickpeas.

Preparation methods:

1. Give the lentils a good rinse, then set them aside.
2. Warm up the olive oil in a big pot over medium heat.
3. Add the grated ginger, minced garlic, and chopped onion. Sauté the food until it becomes tender.
4. Add the sliced carrots, chopped bell peppers, and cauliflower florets and stir. Simmer the veggies for a few minutes, or until they begin to get tender.
5. Add the tomato paste, turmeric, cumin, coriander, curry powder, rinsed lentils, and salt & pepper. Toss to evenly distribute the spices throughout the lentils and veggies.
6. After adding the coconut milk, boil the mixture.
7. After lowering the heat and covering the saucepan, simmer the lentils and vegetables for around 25 to 30 minutes, or until they become soft.
8. Tailor the seasoning to your personal preference.

Dessert and Snacks Recipes

Healthy dessert and snacks that support well-being.

Avocado with Chocolate Mousse

Cooking time: 5 minutes

Portion size: Half a cup.

Ingredients:

- Avocado
- powdered cocoa
- Almond milk
- extract from vanilla

Nutritional value:

High in antioxidants, fiber, and good fats.

Recipes substitute:

Preparation methods:

1. Peel and pit the avocado.
2. Blend together avocado, almond milk, cocoa powder, and vanilla essence using a blender.
3. Blend till creamy and smooth.

Berry and Yogurt Parfait

Cooking time: There is no need to cook.   **Portion size:** 1 cup.

Ingredients:

- Greek yogurt
- Various berries
- chopped almonds

Nutritional value:

High in protein, vitamins, and antioxidants

Recipes substitute:

Preparation methods:

1. Arrange Greek yogurt, chopped nuts, and mixed berries in a bowl or glass.
2. Layers can be repeated as needed.

Pudding with Chia Seeds

Cooking time: Five minutes plus overnight   **Portion size:** 1 cup.

Ingredients:

- Chia seeds
- Almond milk
- extract from vanilla

Nutritional value:

Rich in fiber, protein, and omega-3 fatty acids.

Recipes substitute:

Preparation methods:

1. Slice the cucumber into rounds.
2. Present cucumber slices alongside a serving of hummus.

Hummus on Cucumber Slices

Cooking time: There is no need to cook.   **Portion size:** 1 cup.

Ingredients:
- Cucumber
- Hummus

Nutritional value:

High in fiber, low in calories, and hydrating.

Recipes substitute:

Preparation methods:
1. Slice the cucumber into rounds.
2. Present cucumber slices alongside a serving of hummus.

Spiced Roasted Chickpeas

Cooking time: 30 minutes.

Portion size: 1/2 cup.

Ingredients:
- Garbanzo beans
- Spices (paprika, cumin, garlic powder) and olive oil

Nutritional value:

High in fiber and protein.

Recipes substitute:

Preparation methods:
1. Turn oven temperature up to 400°F (200°C).
2. Rinse the chickpeas and pat dry.
3. Coat the chickpeas with spices and olive oil by tossing them.
4. Roast for 25 to 30 minutes, or until crispy, in the oven.

Apple Chips Baked

Cooking time: 2 or 3 hours for cooking.   **Portion size:** 1 cup.

Ingredients:
- Apples

Nutritional value:

Rich in vitamins, fiber, and low in calories.

Recipes substitute:

Preparation methods:
1. Turn oven temperature up to 200°F, or 95°C.
2. Cut apples into thin slices.
3. Slices should be arranged and dusted with cinnamon on a baking pan.
4. Bake until crisp, two to three hours.

Pesto with Zucchini Noodles

Cooking time: 10 minutes

Portion size: 1 cup.

Ingredients:

- Zucchini
- Sugar-free basil pesto
- Noodles made from spiralized zucchini

Nutritional value:

Rich in vitamins and good fats, low in carbohydrates.

Recipes substitute:

Preparation methods:

1. Toss with sugar-free pesto made with basil.
2. Serve cold or very briefly sautéed.

Cucumber and Strawberry Salad

Cooking time: There is no need to cook.   **Portion size:** 1 cup.

Ingredients:

- strawberries
- Cucumber
- mint leaves

Nutritional value:

High in vitamins, hydrating, and low in calories.

Recipes substitute:

Preparation methods:

1. Combine all ingredients in a bowl.
2. Form into bouncy balls.
3. Let it cool for half an hour before serving.

Berry
and Coconut Yogurt

Cooking time: There is no need to cook.   **Portion size:** 1 cup.

Ingredients:

- Unsweetened coconut yogurt.
- Various berries
- Coconut flakes without sugar

Nutritional value:

Rich in antioxidants and probiotics, devoid of dairy.

Recipes substitute:

Preparation methods:

1. Transfer coconut yogurt into a bowl using a spoon.
2. Add mixed berries and coconut flakes over top.

Popped Cauliflower

Cooking time: 20 minutes.　　　　**Portion size:** 1 cup.

Ingredients:
- Florets of cauliflower
- Garlic powder, paprika, and turmeric added to olive oil for seasoning

Nutritional value:

Rich in vitamin C, high in fiber, and low in calories.

Recipes substitute:

Preparation methods:
1. Toss cauliflower with seasonings and olive oil.
2. Bake until the food is golden brown.

Mango-Cucumber Salsa

Cooking time: There is no need to cook.   **Portion size:** 1 cup.

Ingredients:
- mango
- cucumber
- Onion red
- Lime juice

Nutritional value:

Hydrating, vitamin-rich, and low in calories.

Recipes substitute:

Preparation methods:
1. Dice the red onion, cucumber, and mango.
2. Add freshly squeezed lime juice and mix.

Trail Mix with Pumpkin Seeds

Cooking time: There is no need to cook.   **Portion size:** 1/4 cup.

Ingredients:
- Seeds from pumpkin
- Almonds
- Dried unsweetened cranberries

Nutritional value:

High in antioxidants, fiber, and protein, this food has a high nutritional value.

Recipes substitute:

Preparation methods:
1. Mix together cranberries, almonds, and pumpkin seeds.
2. Mix thoroughly and transfer to snack-sized bags.

Slaw with carrots and cabbage

Cooking time: There is no need to cook.   **Portion size:** 1 cup.

Ingredients:
- shredded green cabbage
- chopped carrot
- vinegar made from apples

Nutritional value:

Rich in fiber, vitamin A, and low in calories.

Recipes substitute:

Preparation methods:
1. Combine carrot and cabbage.
2. Use apple cider vinegar as a dressing.

Stuffed Mushrooms with Feta and Spinach

Cooking time: 15 minutes.

Portion size: Four mushrooms make up one portion.

Ingredients:

- Mushrooms
- Fresh spinach and Feta cheese

Nutritional value:

Rich in vitamins and iron, low in calories.

Recipes substitute:

Preparation methods:

1. Cut off the stems from the mushrooms and pack with feta and sautéed spinach.
2. Bake the mushrooms until they become soft.

Pasta with Basil Tomatoes

Cooking time: There is no need to cook.   **Portion size:** 1 cup.

Ingredients:

- Tomatoes
- Fresh basil
- Olive oil

Nutritional value:

Heart-healthy fats, vitamins, and low calorie content.

Recipes substitute:

Preparation methods:

1. Dice tomatoes and finely chop fresh basil.
2. Serve atop slices of cucumber after tossing with olive oil.

Mint
and Watermelon Salad

Cooking time: There is no need to cook.   **Portion size:** 1 cup.

Ingredients:
- Watermelon
- mint leaves that are fresh

Nutritional value:

High in vitamins, low in calories, and hydrating.

Recipes substitute:

Preparation methods:
1. Chop mint leaves and cube watermelon as part of the preparation process.
2. Toss and chill before serving.

Chips made with eggplant

Cooking time: 25 minutes.   **Portion size:** 1 cup.

Ingredients:
- eggplant
- Extra virgin olive oil and Italian spice

Nutritional value:

Rich in antioxidants, high in fiber, and low in calories.

Recipes substitute:

Preparation methods:
1. Cut eggplant into slices and mix with seasoning and olive oil.
2. Bake in the oven until crispy.

Coconut Chia Popsicles with Blueberries

Cooking time: 4 hours (frozen).

Portion size: 1 popsicle

Ingredients:
- Blueberries
- Water from coconuts
- Chia seeds

Nutritional value:

Hydrating, rich in antioxidants, and low in calories.

Recipes substitute:

Preparation methods:
1. Blend chia seeds, coconut water, and blueberries.
2. Fill popsicle molds, then freeze.

CONCLUSION

Adopting a sugar-free diet is a transformative journey towards long-term health rather than just a short-term adjustment.

You've learned that eliminating refined sugars doesn't have to mean sacrificing flavor as you've experimented with the many mouthwatering dishes in this cookbook. Rather, it provides access to a plethora of healthful components that support the body and the spirit.

Recall that the goal of this trip is balance, not deprivation. It's about discovering happiness in complete, nutrient-dense foods that support general health, nourish your body, and increase your energy. No matter how tiny the victory, acknowledge it and welcome the process of learning.

Now that you know sugar substitutes and innovative culinary methods, you have all you need to establish a long-term, sugar-free lifestyle. This cookbook can serve as a roadmap, but it can also serve as a launchpad for your creative cooking.

Encourage your loved ones to follow you on your journey to improved health by imparting your acquired knowledge to them. As we come to the end of this cookbook, think of it as a partner on your continuing road to a bright, sugar-free life rather than merely a compilation of recipes.

I hope that your kitchen remains a place where happiness and health coexist, and that every meal serves as evidence of the influence of thoughtful decisions. Cheers to a life full of taste, devoid of needless sugar, and bursting with the energy that comes from giving your body the love and care it deserves. To your well-being and culinary explorations!

Happy Cooking!

CHAPTER 4
Meal Planner Journal

Weekly Meal planner journal

Dates

	BREAKFAST	LUNCH	DINNER	SNACKS
MON				
TUE				
WED				
THU				
FRI				
SAT				
SUN				

Shopping list

_____
_____
_____
_____
_____
_____

Note:

Weekly Meal planner journal

Dates

	BREAKFAST	LUNCH	DINNER	SNACKS
MON				
TUE				
WED				
THU				
FRI				
SAT				
SUN				

Shopping list

_____

_____

_____

_____

_____

_____

Note:

Weekly Meal planner journal

Dates

	BREAKFAST	LUNCH	DINNER	SNACKS
MON				
TUE				
WED				
THU				
FRI				
SAT				
SUN				

Shopping list

_____
_____
_____
_____
_____
_____

Note:

Dates

	BREAKFAST	LUNCH	DINNER	SNACKS
MON				
TUE				
WED				
THU				
FRI				
SAT				
SUN				

Shopping list

_____
_____
_____
_____
_____
_____

Note:

Weekly Meal planner journal

Dates

	BREAKFAST	LUNCH	DINNER	SNACKS
MON				
TUE				
WED				
THU				
FRI				
SAT				
SUN				

Shopping list

_____

_____

_____

_____

_____

Note:

Weekly Meal planner journal

Dates

	BREAKFAST	LUNCH	DINNER	SNACKS
MON				
TUE				
WED				
THU				
FRI				
SAT				
SUN				

Shopping list

_____
_____
_____
_____
_____
_____

Note:

Weekly Meal planner journal

Dates

	BREAKFAST	LUNCH	DINNER	SNACKS
MON				
TUE				
WED				
THU				
FRI				
SAT				
SUN				

Shopping list

_____
_____
_____
_____
_____
_____

Note:

Weekly Meal planner journal

Dates

	BREAKFAST	LUNCH	DINNER	SNACKS
MON				
TUE				
WED				
THU				
FRI				
SAT				
SUN				

Shopping list

_____
_____
_____
_____
_____
_____

Note:

Weekly Meal planner journal

Dates

	BREAKFAST	LUNCH	DINNER	SNACKS
MON				
TUE				
WED				
THU				
FRI				
SAT				
SUN				

Shopping list

_____
_____
_____
_____
_____
_____

Note:

Weekly Meal planner journal

Dates

	BREAKFAST	LUNCH	DINNER	SNACKS
MON				
TUE				
WED				
THU				
FRI				
SAT				
SUN				

Shopping list

_____
_____
_____
_____
_____
_____

Note:

Weekly Meal planner journal

Dates

	BREAKFAST	LUNCH	DINNER	SNACKS
MON				
TUE				
WED				
THU				
FRI				
SAT				
SUN				

Shopping list

_____
_____
_____
_____
_____
_____

Note:

Weekly Meal planner journal

Dates

	BREAKFAST	LUNCH	DINNER	SNACKS
MON				
TUE				
WED				
THU				
FRI				
SAT				
SUN				

Shopping list

_____
_____
_____
_____
_____
_____

Note:

Weekly Meal planner journal

Dates

	BREAKFAST	LUNCH	DINNER	SNACKS
MON				
TUE				
WED				
THU				
FRI				
SAT				
SUN				

Shopping list

_____
_____
_____
_____
_____
_____

Note:

Weekly Meal planner journal

Dates

	BREAKFAST	LUNCH	DINNER	SNACKS
MON				
TUE				
WED				
THU				
FRI				
SAT				
SUN				

Shopping list

_____
_____
_____
_____
_____
_____

Note:

Weekly Meal planner journal

Dates

	BREAKFAST	LUNCH	DINNER	SNACKS
MON				
TUE				
WED				
THU				
FRI				
SAT				
SUN				

Shopping list

_____
_____
_____
_____
_____
_____

Note:

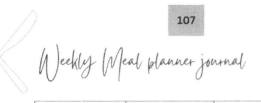

Weekly Meal planner journal

Dates

	BREAKFAST	LUNCH	DINNER	SNACKS
MON				
TUE				
WED				
THU				
FRI				
SAT				
SUN				

Shopping list

_____
_____
_____
_____
_____
_____

Note:

 Weekly Meal planner journal

Dates

	BREAKFAST	LUNCH	DINNER	SNACKS
MON				
TUE				
WED				
THU				
FRI				
SAT				
SUN				

Shopping list

_____
_____
_____
_____
_____

Note:

Weekly Meal planner journal

Dates

	BREAKFAST	LUNCH	DINNER	SNACKS
MON				
TUE				
WED				
THU				
FRI				
SAT				
SUN				

Shopping list

_____
_____
_____
_____
_____
_____

Note:

Weekly Meal planner journal

Dates

	BREAKFAST	LUNCH	DINNER	SNACKS
MON				
TUE				
WED				
THU				
FRI				
SAT				
SUN				

Shopping list

_____

_____

_____

_____

_____

_____

Note:

Weekly Meal planner journal

Dates

	BREAKFAST	LUNCH	DINNER	SNACKS
MON				
TUE				
WED				
THU				
FRI				
SAT				
SUN				

Shopping list

_____
_____
_____
_____
_____
_____

Note:

Weekly Meal planner journal

Dates

	BREAKFAST	LUNCH	DINNER	SNACKS
MON				
TUE				
WED				
THU				
FRI				
SAT				
SUN				

Shopping list

_____
_____
_____
_____
_____
_____

Note:

Weekly Meal planner journal

Dates

	BREAKFAST	LUNCH	DINNER	SNACKS
MON				
TUE				
WED				
THU				
FRI				
SAT				
SUN				

Shopping list

_____
_____
_____
_____
_____
_____

Note:

Weekly Meal planner journal

Dates

	BREAKFAST	LUNCH	DINNER	SNACKS
MON				
TUE				
WED				
THU				
FRI				
SAT				
SUN				

Shopping list

_____

_____

_____

_____

_____

_____

Note:

Weekly Meal planner journal

Dates

	BREAKFAST	LUNCH	DINNER	SNACKS
MON				
TUE				
WED				
THU				
FRI				
SAT				
SUN				

Shopping list

Note:

Weekly Meal planner journal

Dates

	BREAKFAST	LUNCH	DINNER	SNACKS
MON				
TUE				
WED				
THU				
FRI				
SAT				
SUN				

Shopping list

_____
_____
_____
_____
_____
_____

Note:

Weekly Meal planner journal

Dates

	BREAKFAST	LUNCH	DINNER	SNACKS
MON				
TUE				
WED				
THU				
FRI				
SAT				
SUN				

Shopping list

_____
_____
_____
_____
_____
_____

Note:

Weekly Meal planner journal

Dates

	BREAKFAST	LUNCH	DINNER	SNACKS
MON				
TUE				
WED				
THU				
FRI				
SAT				
SUN				

Shopping list
_____
_____
_____
_____
_____
_____

Note:

Weekly Meal planner journal

Dates

	BREAKFAST	LUNCH	DINNER	SNACKS
MON				
TUE				
WED				
THU				
FRI				
SAT				
SUN				

Shopping list

_____
_____
_____
_____
_____
_____

Note:

Weekly Meal planner journal

Dates

	BREAKFAST	LUNCH	DINNER	SNACKS
MON				
TUE				
WED				
THU				
FRI				
SAT				
SUN				

Shopping list

_____
_____
_____
_____
_____
_____

Note:

Weekly Meal planner journal

Dates

	BREAKFAST	LUNCH	DINNER	SNACKS
MON				
TUE				
WED				
THU				
FRI				
SAT				
SUN				

Shopping list

_____
_____
_____
_____
_____
_____

Note:

Made in the USA
Monee, IL
05 May 2025

16921559R00069